Typed Resource Definitions

Incident Management Resources

FEMA 508-2

July 2005

Background	The National Mutual Aid and Resource Management Initiative supports the National Incident Management System (NIMS) by establishing a comprehensive, integrated national mutual aid and resource management system that provides the basis to type, order, and track all (Federal, State, and local) response assets.
Resource Typing	For ease of ordering and tracking, response assets need to be categorized via resource typing. Resource typing is the categorization and description of resources that are commonly exchanged in disasters via mutual aid, by capacity and/or capability. Through resource typing, disciplines examine resources and identify the capabilities of a resource's components (i.e., personnel, equipment, training). During a disaster, an emergency manager knows what capability a resource needs to have to respond efficiently and effectively. Resource typing definitions will help define resource capabilities for ease of ordering and mobilization during a disaster. As a result of the resource typing process, a resource's capability is readily defined and an emergency manager is able to effectively and efficiently request and receive resources through mutual aid during times of disaster.
Web Site	For more information, you can also refer to the National Mutual Aid and Resource Management Web site located at:

http://www.fema.gov/nims/mutual_aid.shtm.

Supersedure	This document replaces *Emergency Management Resources*, dated May 2005
Changes	EMAC Advance Team table deleted pending complete rewrite. Document Title renamed. Table categories changed to comply with NIMS category list.

Table of Contents

RESOURCE:	Airborne Communications Relay Team (Fixed-Wing)			
CATEGORY:	Resource Management		**KIND:**	Aircraft
MINIMUM CAPABILITIES:				
COMPONENT	METRIC	TYPE I	TYPE II	TYPE III	TYPE IV	OTHER

COMPONENT	METRIC	TYPE I	TYPE II	TYPE III	TYPE IV	OTHER
Personnel	See Note 1 See Note 2	Instrument-rated (IFR) pilot/co-pilot	Non-instrument rated pilot/co-pilot	Instrument rated (IFR) pilot/co-pilot	Non-instrument rated (VFR) pilot/co-pilot	
Equipment	See Note 3	Same as Type IV	Same as Type IV	Capable of operations up to 10,000'	Capable of operations up to 10,000' MSL Carries (provided) airborne repeater (or cross-band repeater) for hands-off communications relay	
Aircraft	Fixed-Wing See Note 4	Same as Type III	No-overcast and clear-above flight conditions	Flight possible through and in overcast conditions	Flight possible through overcast and clear-above conditions	

COMMENTS: Team provides airborne communications relay using fixed-wing platforms to support Federal, State, and local emergency needs. Relays are primarily conducted through aircrews, but can also be accomplished through electronic repeaters carried aboard CAP aircraft. Varying levels of specialized management support and command/control capabilities are included in team structures. Notes: Airborne repeaters and crossband repeaters must be provided by the requesting agency, but team will install.

Source: Washington State Civil Air Patrol

Note 1: Crew members capable of at least 8 hours of flying per day and 14-hour duty day. Number of certified pilots, equipment operators, and technicians needed to maintain communications platform depending on size and capability of aircraft.

Note 2: Trained communicator on board to "in-person" relay communications ("traffic") from sender to receiver on miscellaneous frequencies or channels, including FCC and NTIA controlled frequencies.

Note 3: Airborne platform for (voice, data, images) communications relay and airborne repeater traffic. Enables VHF/UHF communications where ground-to-ground contact is impossible.

Note 4: Fixed-Wing single-engine or twin-engine aircraft (i.e., Cessna C182, C182RG, C206, TU206). Requires access to fuel supply and fueling points, and routine maintenance facilities and supplies for extended deployments.

RESOURCE:	Airborne Communications Relay (Fixed-Wing) (CAP)			
CATEGORY:	Resource Management	**KIND:**	Aircraft	

MINIMUM CAPABILITIES:					
COMPONENT	**METRIC**	**TYPE I**	**TYPE II**	**TYPE III**	**TYPE IV**	**OTHER**
Vehicle	Fixed-Wing Aircraft	Same as Type II	IFR-Capable Fixed-Wing CAP Aircraft	Fixed-Wing CAP Aircraft	Fixed-Wing Aircraft (member owned)	
Vehicle	Capacity	Same as Type II	Same as Type III	Same as Type IV	2-4 passengers with cargo not to exceed design specification of aircraft	
Equipment	Flight Suit	Same as Type II	Same as Type III	Same as Type IV	Appropriate level of PPE	
Equipment	Communications	Same as Type III plus Airborne Repeater capable of patching across multiple operating radio bands	Same as Type III plus Airborne Repeater supporting Federal frequency assignments	Same as Type IV plus: VHF Radios	Standard FAA FM Radio	
Personnel	Training & Ratings	Same as Type II	Pilot – Private Pilot (instrument) or higher certificate and complete unit certification program	Same as Type IV plus: Instrument rating desired, but not required	Pilot – Private Pilot or higher certificate and complete unit certification program	
Personnel	Crew Availability	Same as Type II	Same as Type III	Same as Type IV	Aircrew(s) available for short duration operations (1 week or less)	
Personnel	Management Support - Coordination Capabilities	Same as Type II	Incident staff capable of managing air operations branch	Incident staff capable of supporting independent flight release	Unit-level flight release	

COMMENTS:	Aircrews can work a maximum of 12-hour shifts, depending on individual unit policies and procedures. Crew availability does not require continuous availability of specific personnel, only that crews are available to those specifications.
	Aircraft will be maintained in accordance with Federal Aviation Administration Regulations.
	Aircraft will be expected to operate out of established airfield with paved runways.
	Aircrews will indicate fueling and runway requirements for the aircraft provided.

FEMA

RESOURCE:	Airborne Transport Team (Fixed-Wing)				
CATEGORY:	Transportation (ESF #1)		KIND:	Aircraft	
MINIMUM CAPABILITIES:		TYPE I	TYPE II	TYPE III	TYPE IV	OTHER
COMPONENT	METRIC					
Personnel	Crew members See Note 1	Instrument-rated (IFR) pilot/co-pilot	Non-instrument rated pilot/co-pilot (1 pilot required only)	Instrument-rated (IFR) pilot/co-pilot (pilot and co-pilot required)	Non-instrument rated pilot/co-pilot (1 pilot required only)	
Personnel	Number of passengers	Maximum 2 additional	Maximum 3	Maximum 1	Maximum 2	
Aircraft	Fixed-Wing See Note 2 See Note 3	Airborne transport capable of operations up to 10,000' MSL Flight possible through and in overcast conditions (instrument meteorological conditions)	Airborne transport capable of operations up to 10,000' MSL Visual meteorological conditions only	Airborne transport capable of operations up to 10,000' MSL Flight possible through and in overcast conditions (instrument meteorological conditions)	Visual meteorological conditions only	
Aircraft	Cargo	Carries up to 350 lbs.	Carries up to 500 lbs.	Carries up to 200 lbs.	Carries up to 350 lbs.	
COMMENTS:	Team provides limited airborne transportation and emergency airlift to support Federal, State, and local agency needs using light fixed-wing platforms owned by CAP. Varying levels of specialized management support and command/control capabilities are included in team structures. Source: *Washington State Civil Air Patrol* **Note 1:** Crew members capable of at least 8 hours of flying per day and 14-hour duty day. Number of certified pilots, equipment operators, and technicians needed depends on size and capability of aircraft. **Note 2:** Fixed-Wing single-engine or twin-engine aircraft capable of 120 knots (130 mph) at cruise (i.e., Cessna C182, C182RG, C206, TU206). Capable of point-to-point transport into short airfields; Capable of eye-in-the-sky coordination of tactical teams on the ground and photo/imaging; GPS guided. **Note 3:** Requires access to fuel supply and fueling points, and routine maintenance facilities and supplies for extended deployments.					

Communications Support Team (CAP)

RESOURCE:						
CATEGORY:	Resource Management			**KIND:**	Team	
MINIMUM CAPABILITIES:						
COMPONENT	**METRIC**	**TYPE I**	**TYPE II**	**TYPE III**	**TYPE IV**	**OTHER**
Personnel	Manning	4 radio operators 1 unit leader 1 dedicated technician	3 radio operators 1 unit leader 1 technician on call	2 radio operators 1 unit leader	1 radio operator 1 unit leader	
Equipment	Communications	Mobile FAA FM Radio Mobile and Portable VHF/FM Radios, capable of AES/DES encryption Portable VHF/FM repeater, capable of AES/DES encryption Mobile and Portable UHF/FM Radios, capable of AES/DES encryption Portable UHF/FM repeater, capable of AES/DES encryption Satellite Phone ALE Capable HF Radio HF E-mail Link	Mobile FAA FM Radio Mobile and Portable VHF/FM Radios, capable of DES encryption Portable VHF/FM repeater Mobile and Portable UHF/FM Radios, capable of DES encryption Cell Phone ALE Capable HF Radio	Same as Type IV plus HF Radio	Mobile FAA FM Radio Mobile and Portable VHF/FM Radios Cell Phone	
Team	Availability and Duration	Same as Type II	Extended operations (greater than 1 week)	Same as Type IV	Short duration operations (1 week or less)	
Management Support	Coordination Capabilities	Same as Type II	Same as Type III	Incident staff capable of managing the communications unit	Team management only	
COMMENTS:		Availability does not require continuous availability of specific personnel, only that teams are available to those specifications. Personnel may be rotated in and out of specific team positions. Type IV teams are expected to serve as independent relay points. Type III teams are expected to support local level incident operations. Type II teams are expected to support regional incident operations with multiple agencies. Type I teams are expected to support national incident operations with multiple agencies.				

Critical Incident Stress Management Team

RESOURCE:					
CATEGORY:	Health and Medical (ESF #8)		**KIND:**	Team	
MINIMUM CAPABILITIES:					
COMPONENT	**METRIC**	**TYPE I**	**TYPE II**	**TYPE III**	**TYPE IV**	**OTHER**
Personnel	Number of Team Coordinators	1-2	1	1		
Personnel	Team Coordinator Experience and Comprehension	Experience as supervisor of CISM Team in large-scale disaster situations in home and other States. Has extensive experience in CISM team administration and knowledge of ICISF standards.	Experience as supervisor of CISM Team in medium- to large-scale disaster situations in home State. Has extensive experience in CISM team administration and knowledge of ICISF standards.	Experience as supervisor of CISM Team in small-scale disaster situations in home State. Has experience in CISM team administration and knowledge of ICISF standards.		
Personnel	Team Coordinator Training	Completed certification from the ICISF. Participated in training approved by the ICISF	Completed certification from the ICISF. Participated in training approved by the ICISF	Participated in training approved by the ICISF		
Personnel	Number of team members See Note 1	10-15	2-4	1		
Personnel	Team member experience and comprehension	Experience as part of CISM Team in large-scale disaster situations in home and other States. Has extensive experience in CISM administration and knowledge of ICISF standards.	Experience as part of CISM Team in medium- to large-scale disaster situations in home State. Has extensive experience in CISM administration and knowledge of ICISF standards.	Experience as part of CISM Team in small-scale disaster situations in home State.		
Personnel	Team member training	Completed certification from the ICISF. Participated in training approved by the ICISF	Completed certification from the ICISF. Participated in training approved by the ICISF	Participated in training approved by the ICISF		

FEMA

RESOURCE:	Critical Incident Stress Management Team			
CATEGORY:	Health and Medical (ESF #8)	**KIND:**	Team	
MINIMUM CAPABILITIES:				
COMPONENT	**METRIC**	**TYPE I**	**TYPE II**	**TYPE III**	**TYPE IV**	**OTHER**
Equipment		Laptop with wireless Internet capabilities Satellite/cell phone	Laptop with Internet capabilities Cell phone			
COMMENTS:	**Note 1:** Number of team members based on size of incident and effects on emergency responders; experience, training, and comprehension Team is responsible for the prevention and mitigation of disabling stress among emergency responders in accordance with the standards of the International Critical Incident Stress Foundation (ICISF). Team composition, management, membership and governance varies, but can include psychologists, psychiatrists, social workers, and licensed professional counselors. *Source: International Critical Incident Stress Foundation*				

RESOURCE:	**Donations Coordinator**				
CATEGORY:	Volunteers and Donations (ESF #15), Mass Care (ESF #6)		**KIND:** Personnel		
MINIMUM CAPABILITIES:					
COMPONENT	**METRIC**	**TYPE I**	**TYPE II**	**TYPE III**	**TYPE IV**	**OTHER**

Component	Metric	Type I	Type II	Type III	Type IV	Other
Personnel	Experience and Comprehension See Note 1	Experience in supervisory role in Donation Coordination in three or more federally declared disaster situations in different States. Has extensive experience in working with NVOAD agencies and MOUs. Has organized and supervised Donation Management in a non-federally declared disaster. Has complete working knowledge of IA & PA and VAL functions under FEMA/State agreement. Understands function of long-term recovery committees	Experience in supervisory role in Donation Coordination in a federally declared disaster. Has worked with a State VOAD on organizing donation management on non-federally declared disaster. Aware of IA and VAL functions under FEMA/State Agreement	Experience in working with a federally declared disaster donation coordination effort. Active in VOAD meetings.	Has attended State VOAD meetings	
Personnel	Training	Has TTT-Training and has trained donations management and volunteer coordination.	Has had training in donations management and volunteer coordination.	Has had training in donations management and volunteer coordination	Has had training in donations management and volunteer coordination.	
Equipment		Laptop with wireless Internet capabilities; Satellite or cell phone Standardized donations management program and form templates for personalizing to disaster	Laptop with wireless Internet capabilities; Satellite or cell phone Standardized donations management program and forms	Equipment provided by requesting State	Equipment provided by requesting State	

Donations Coordinator

RESOURCE:					
CATEGORY:	Volunteers and Donations (ESF #15), Mass Care (ESF #6)		**KIND:**	Personnel	
MINIMUM CAPABILITIES:	**TYPE I**	**TYPE II**	**TYPE III**	**TYPE IV**	**OTHER**
COMPONENT **METRIC**	**Note: 1** Number based on size and scope of event and public reaction to event.				
COMMENTS:	Possesses an operational knowledge of all aspects of donations coordination, including management of solicited and unsolicited funds, goods, and services from concerned citizens and private organizations following a catastrophic disaster situation. Interfaces with the other State and local government agencies, the FEMA Donations Coordinator, Non-Governmental Organizations (NGOs), and Volunteer Organizations Active in Disaster (VOAD), such as the American Red Cross, The Salvation Army, and religious organizations as appropriate for the emergency situation. Capable of the physical establishment and operation of the Donations Coordination Center (DCC), which may be part of the Emergency Operations Center (EOC) or other designated location, including facility, data management, and internal operations. Capable of managing donations phone banks, distribution centers, warehousing, and supply systems; and records offers of donated funds, goods, and volunteer services. The Donations Coordination/Management Team Leader determines number of donations coordinators per incident. **Note:** Donations Coordinator is a subsection of a Donations Management Team. Has working knowledge of the Individual Assistance and Public Assistance functions under FEMA/State agreement. Has working knowledge of establishing long-term recovery committees on local levels following events.				

RESOURCE:		Donations Management Personnel/Team			
CATEGORY:	Volunteers and Donations (ESF #15)		KIND:	Team	
MINIMUM CAPABILITIES:					
COMPONENT	METRIC	TYPE I	TYPE II	TYPE III	TYPE IV	OTHER
Personnel	Team Leader Expertise, Training, and Experience	X (See Comments section)				
Personnel	Donations Specialist Training and Experience	X (See Comments section)	X (See Comments section) May be referred to as Donations Strike Team			
COMMENTS:	A donations management team consists of one or two persons trained and experienced in all aspects of donations management. The team will be deployed to a disaster-affected jurisdiction after impact to assist in the organization and operations of local or state donations management in support of the affected jurisdiction. Each Person: Possesses an overall knowledge of all aspects of donations management at all levels. Capable of assisting the jurisdiction (if required) in the establishment of a multiagency warehouse, integration of donated goods and services into the overall disaster supply system, and recommends the establishment of local distribution centers, as necessary. Team Leader: Experienced in actual donations operations. Capable of providing advice on Voluntary Agency/Donations Coordination Team (DCT) coordination. Assists the NGOs, State, and local government in the coordination of joint activities to support donations management operations. Donations Specialist: Possesses an overall knowledge of all aspects of donations management at all levels. Capable of assisting in the physical establishment of the Donations Coordination Center (DCC) and the Phone Bank (if required). This includes facility, data management, and internal operations. Capable of assisting the NGOs, State, and local government in the coordination of joint activities to support donations management operations.				

RESOURCE:	EOC Finance/Administration Section Chief/Coordinator					
CATEGORY:	Resource Management			KIND:	Personnel	
MINIMUM CAPABILITIES:		TYPE I	TYPE II	TYPE III	TYPE IV	OTHER
COMPONENT	METRIC					
Personnel	Experience, Training, and Comprehension	Supervisory role in Finance/Admin in 3 or more federally declared disaster situations in different States. Has organized and supervised subunits of Section in a federally and/or non-federally declared disaster. Has extensive experience and training in IC system	Supervisory role in Finance/Admin in a federally declared disaster situation in home and/or other State. Has organized and supervised subunits of Section in a non-federally declared disaster in home State. Has experience and training in IC system	Training and/or experience in Finance/Admin for non-federally declared disaster situations in home State. Has training in IC system		
Equipment		Laptop with wireless Internet capabilities; Satellite/cell phone; Standardized forms commonly used in the execution of this function	Laptop with Internet capabilities; Satellite/cell phone; Standardized forms commonly used in the execution of this function	Equipment provided by requesting State: Laptop, comm., and standardized forms commonly used in the execution of this function		
COMMENTS:	Individual at the EOC responsible for tracking incident costs and reimbursement accounting, and coordinating/administering support for EOC personnel during disaster operations. This function is part of the standardized ICS structure per the National Incident Management System. If situation warrants, chief/coordinator oversees subunits of this function to include Compensation/Claims, Procurement, Cost, and Time. (See **Figure 1.**) When there is a specific need for financial reimbursement (individual and agency or department), and/or administrative services to support incident management activities, a Finance/Administration Section is established. Under the ICS, not all agencies will require such assistance. In large, complex scenarios involving significant funding originating from multiple sources, the Finance/Administrative Section is an essential part of the ICS. In addition to monitoring multiple sources of funds, the Section Chief must track and report to the IC the financial "burn rate" as the incident progresses. This allows the IC to forecast the need for additional funds before operations are affected negatively. This is particularly important if significant operational assets are under contract from the private sector. The Section Chief may also need to monitor cost expenditures to ensure statutory rules that apply are met. Close coordination with the Planning Section and Logistics Section is also essential so that operational records can be reconciled with financial documents. Note that, in some cases, only one specific function may be required (e.g., cost analysis), which a technical specialist in the Planning Section could provide. The Finance/Administration Section Chief will determine, given current and anticipated future requirements, the need for establishing specific subordinate units. In some of the functional areas (e.g., procurement), an actual unit need not be established if it would consist of only one person. In such a case, a procurement technical specialist would be assigned in the Planning Section instead. Because of the specialized nature of finance functions, the Section Chief should come from the agency that has the greatest requirement for this support. The Section Chief may have a deputy. *Source: National Incident Management System, March 2004*					

FEMA

RESOURCE:	EOC Finance/Administration Section Chief/Coordinator				
CATEGORY:	Resource Management		KIND:	Personnel	
MINIMUM CAPABILITIES:					
COMPONENT	METRIC	TYPE I	TYPE II	TYPE III	TYPE IV	OTHER

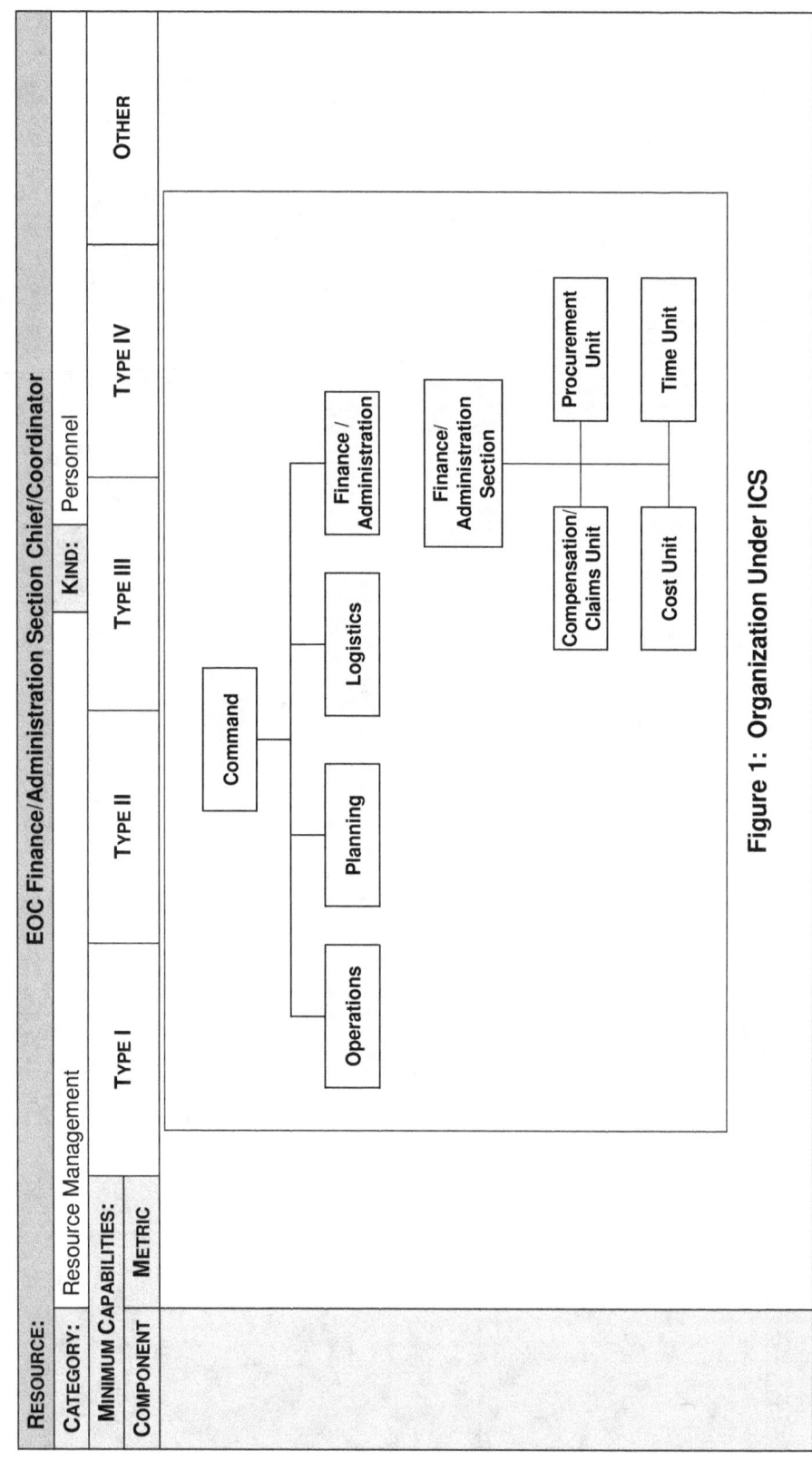

Figure 1: Organization Under ICS

RESOURCE:	EOC Management Support Team				
CATEGORY:	Resource Management	**KIND:**	Team		
MINIMUM CAPABILITIES:					
COMPONENT	**METRIC**	**TYPE I**	**TYPE II**	**TYPE III**	**TYPE IV**	**OTHER**
Personnel	Information Officer	Yes	Yes	Yes	Yes	
Personnel	Liaison Officer	Yes	Yes	Yes	Yes	
Personnel	Safety Officer	Yes	Yes			
Personnel	Incident Commander See Note 1	Optional	Optional	Optional		
Personnel	Administrative Aide	Yes				
COMMENTS:	Provides support to an Incident Commander. Typically comprised of an Information Officer, Liaison Officer, Safety Officer, and Administrative Aide, although some functions may be optional.					
	Note 1: An Incident Commander is an optional member of the team, since it is assumed that an Incident Command/lead has already been established under which these support functions will operate. Refer also to "Incident Management Team."					
	Information Officer: The Information Officer is responsible for developing and releasing information about the incident to the news media, to incident personnel, and to other appropriate agencies and organizations. Only one Information Officer will be assigned for each incident, including incidents operating under Unified Command and multijurisdictional incidents. The Information Officer may have assistants as necessary, and the assistants may also represent assisting agencies or jurisdictions.					
	Liaison Officer: Incidents that are multijurisdictional, or have several agencies involved, may require the establishment of the Liaison Officer position on the Command Staff. Only one Liaison Officer will be assigned for each incident, including incidents operating under Unified Command and multijurisdictional incidents. The Liaison Officer may have assistants as necessary, and the assistants may also represent assisting agencies or jurisdictions. The Liaison Officer is the contact for the personnel assigned to the incident by assisting or cooperating agencies. These are personnel other than those on direct tactical assignments or those involved in a Unified Command.					
	Safety Officer: The Safety Officer's function is to develop and recommend measures for assuring personnel safety, and to assess and/or anticipate hazardous and unsafe situations. Only one Safety Officer will be assigned for each incident. The Safety Officer may have assistants as necessary, and the assistants may also represent assisting agencies or jurisdictions. Safety assistants may have specific responsibilities such as air operations, hazardous materials, etc.					
	Administrative Aide: The Administrative Aide's function is to provide administrative/secretarial support to the EOC Management Support Team. Responsibilities include keeping official minutes of team meetings, receiving phone calls to the EOC, making meeting arrangements, and other duties as needed.					
	Source: FIRESCOPE, California Department of Emergency Services, 2001; Phoenix Fireground, City of Phoenix Fire Department, 2002					

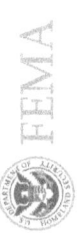

FEMA

RESOURCE:	EOC Operations Section Chief				
CATEGORY:	Resource Management			KIND:	Personnel
MINIMUM CAPABILITIES:		TYPE I	TYPE II	TYPE III	TYPE IV	OTHER
COMPONENT	METRIC					
Personnel	Experience, Training, and Comprehension	Supervisory role in Operations Section in 3 or more federally declared disaster situations in different States. Has organized and supervised subunits of Section in a federally and/or non-federally declared disaster. Has extensive experience and training in IC system	Supervisory role in Operations Section in a federally declared disaster situation in home and/or other State. Has organized and supervised subunits of Section in a non-federally declared disaster in home State. Has experience and training in IC system	Training and/or experience in Operations for non-federally declared disaster situations in home State. Has training in IC system		
Equipment		Laptop with wireless Internet capabilities; Satellite/cell phone; Standardized forms commonly used in the execution of this function	Laptop with Internet capabilities; Satellite/cell phone; Standardized forms commonly used in the execution of this function	Equipment provided by requesting State: Laptop, comm., and standardized forms commonly used in the execution of this function		
COMMENTS:	Individual at the EOC responsible for managing tactical operations at the incident site directed toward reducing the immediate hazard, saving lives and property, establishing situation control, and restoring normal conditions; responsible for the delivery and coordination of disaster assistance programs and services, including emergency assistance, human services assistance, and infrastructure assistance; and oversight of subunits of Operations Section, including Branches, Division/Groups and Resources as warranted. (See **Figure 2**.) The Operations Section Chief directly manages all incident tactical activities and implements the IAP. The Operations Section Chief may have one or more deputies (preferably from other agencies in multijurisdictional incidents). Deputies will be qualified to a similar level as the Operations Section Chief. An Operations Section Chief should be designated for each operational period and will have direct involvement in the preparation of the IAP for the period of responsibility. Source: *National Incident Management System, March 2004*					

FEMA

RESOURCE:	EOC Operations Section Chief			
CATEGORY:	Resource Management		KIND:	Personnel
MINIMUM CAPABILITIES:				
COMPONENT	METRIC	TYPE I	TYPE II	TYPE III	TYPE IV	OTHER

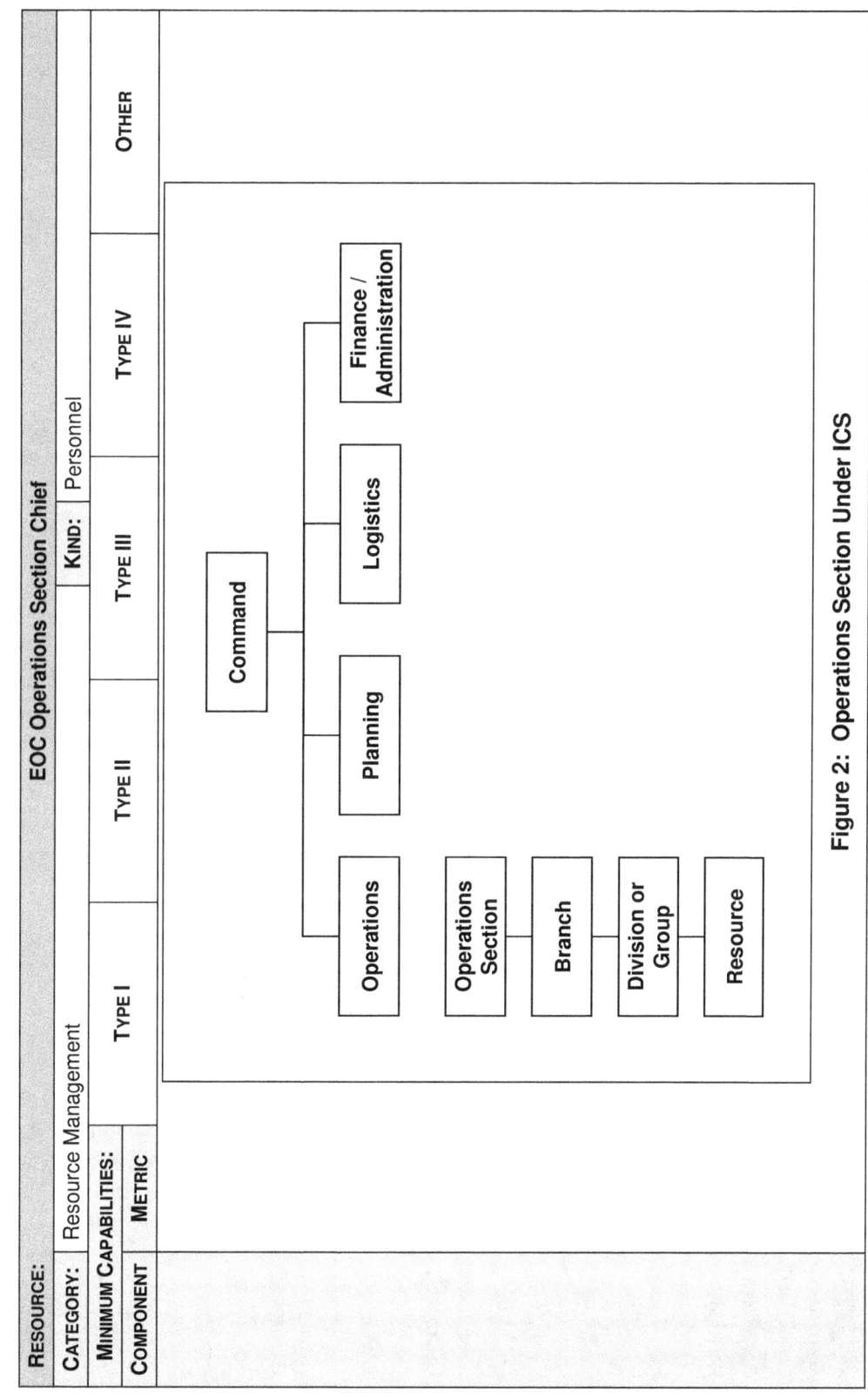

Figure 2: Operations Section Under ICS

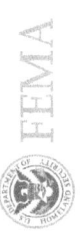

RESOURCE:		EOC Planning Section Chief			
CATEGORY:	Resource Management			**KIND:** Personnel	
MINIMUM CAPABILITIES:		**TYPE I**	**TYPE II**	**TYPE III**	**TYPE IV**	**OTHER**
COMPONENT	**METRIC**					
Personnel	Experience, Training, and Comprehension	Supervisory role in Planning Section in 3 or more federally declared disaster situations in different States. Has organized and supervised subunits of Section in a federally and/or non-federally declared disaster. Has extensive experience and training in IC system	Supervisory role in Planning Section in a federally declared disaster situation in home and/or other State. Has organized and supervised subunits of Section in a non-federally declared disaster in home State. Has experience and training in IC system	Training and/or experience in Planning for non-federally declared disaster situations in home State. Has training in IC system		
Equipment		Laptop with wireless Internet capabilities Satellite/cell phone Standardized forms commonly used in the execution of this function	Laptop with Internet capabilities Satellite/cell phone Standardized forms commonly used in the execution of this function	Equipment provided by requesting State: Laptop, communications, and standardized forms commonly used in the execution of this function		
COMMENTS:	Individual at the EOC who oversees all incident-related data gathering and analysis regarding incident operations and assigned resources, develops alternatives for tactical operations, conducts planning meetings, and prepares the IAP for each operational period. (See **Figure 3.**) The Planning Section is responsible for collecting, evaluating, and disseminating tactical information pertaining to the incident. This section maintains information and intelligence on the current and forecasted situation, as well as the status of resources assigned to the incident. The Planning Section prepares and documents IAPs and incident maps and gathers and disseminates information and intelligence critical to the incident. The Planning Section has four primary units (Resources, Situation, Demobilization, and Documentation) and may include a number of technical specialists to assist in evaluating the situation and forecasting requirements for additional personnel and equipment. *Source: National Incident Management System, March 2004*				

EOC Planning Section Chief

RESOURCE:				
CATEGORY:	Resource Management		**KIND:** Personnel	
MINIMUM CAPABILITIES:				
COMPONENT	**METRIC**	**TYPE I**	**TYPE II**	**TYPE III**	**TYPE IV**	**OTHER**

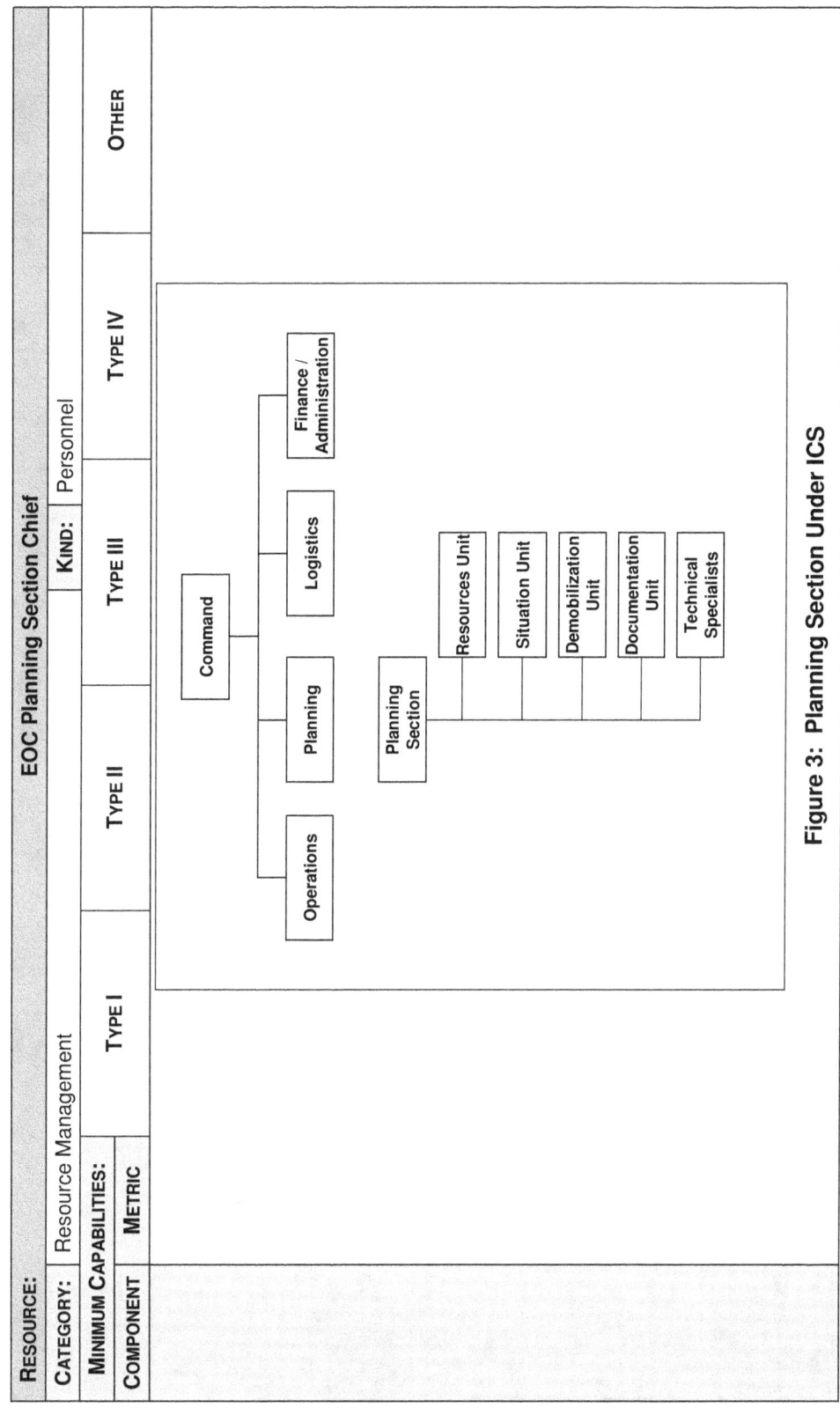

Figure 3: Planning Section Under ICS

FEMA

Evacuation Coordination Team

RESOURCE:	Evacuation Coordination Team				
CATEGORY:	Transportation (ESF #1)		**KIND:**	Team	
MINIMUM CAPABILITIES:					
COMPONENT	**METRIC**	**TYPE I**	**TYPE II**	**TYPE III**	**TYPE IV**	**OTHER**
Personnel	Number based on size and scope of evacuation activities	1 Evacuation Coordination Team leader 2 emergency management specialists 2 information technology specialists 2 transportation specialists	Same as Type III, plus: 1 emergency management specialist	1 Evacuation Coordination Team leader 1 information technology specialist 1 transportation specialist		
Equipment	Scalable based on number of specialists needed	7 laptop computers with wireless/satellite Internet access See Note 1 See Note 2	4 laptop computers with wireless/satellite Internet access See Note 1 See Note 2	Equipment provided by requesting State		

COMMENTS: Provides support in State and local emergency response efforts by compiling, analyzing, and disseminating traffic-related information that can be used to facilitate the rapid, efficient, and safe evacuation of threatened populations. Primarily operates in the State or local EOC as an extension of ESF #1 – Transportation. The mission of the Evacuation Coordination Team is to provide for the protection of life or property by removing endangered persons and property from potential or actual disaster areas to areas of less danger through the successful execution of evacuation procedures.

Note 1: HURREVAC pre-loaded with requesting community clearance times in EVACDATA folder in HURREVAC.

Note 2: Access to ETIS (obtain appropriate State password upon arrival from the local EOC); 2 satellite/cell phones.

See also Evacuation Liaison Team

RESOURCE:	Evacuation Liaison Team (ELT)				
CATEGORY:	Transportation (ESF #1)	**KIND:** Team			
MINIMUM CAPABILITIES:					
COMPONENT	METRIC	TYPE I	TYPE II	TYPE III	TYPE IV	OTHER
Personnel	Emergency Management Specialist	X See Note 1				
Personnel	Information Technology Specialist	X See Note 1				
Personnel	Department of Transportation Specialist	X See Note 1				
Equipment	Deployment Equipment	Two laptop computers with preloaded Internet access programs; See Note 2 Two telephones (landline or cellular)				
COMMENTS:	Provides support in State and local emergency response efforts by compiling, analyzing, and disseminating traffic-related information that can be used to facilitate the rapid, efficient, and safe evacuation of threatened populations. Primarily operates in the State or local EOC as an extension of ESF #1—Transportation. Variations may exist according to level of experience among team members. **Note 1:** Training, Certification (where available), and Experience; Scalable based on number of specialists needed **Note 2:** HURREVAC loaded (with requesting community clearance times in EVACDATA folder in HURREVAC); Internet browser (Explorer preferred); access to ETIS (obtain appropriate state password upon arrival from the local EOC). *Source: ELT draft profile, submitted by State of Florida, Division of Emergency Management, April 2003*					

RESOURCE:	Incident Management Team				
CATEGORY:	Resource Management		**KIND:**	Team	
MINIMUM CAPABILITIES:		**TYPE I**	**TYPE II**	**TYPE III**	**TYPE IV**	**OTHER**
COMPONENT	**METRIC**					
Personnel	Incident Commander	Yes	Yes	Yes	Yes	
Personnel	Operations Section Chief	Yes	Yes	Yes	Yes	
Personnel	Planning Section Chief	Yes	Yes	Yes		
Personnel	Logistics Section Chief	Yes	Yes	Yes		
Personnel	Finance/Admin Section Chief	Yes	Yes	Yes	Yes	
Personnel	Specialized Functions (i.e., HazMat, Insurance, etc.)	Yes	Optional	Optional	Optional	

COMMENTS:

A command team comprised of the Incident Commander, appropriate command and general staff personnel assigned to an incident. (*Source: FIRESCOPE*)

Components and Capabilities: Variations may also be based on level and type of disaster experience. (i.e., local event experience vs. national event experience).

The Incident Commander's responsibility is the overall management of the incident (to which they are assigned). On most incidents, the command activity is carried out by a single Incident Commander. The Incident Commander is selected by qualifications and experience. The Incident Commander may have a deputy, who may be from the same agency, or from an assisting agency. Deputies may also be used at section and branch levels of the ICS organization. Deputies must have the same qualifications as the person for whom they work, as they must be ready to take over that position at any time. Depending on the extent of the Incident Management team needed, this area of management may also have under its purview an Information Officer, Liaison Officer, Agency Representative(s), and Safety Officer.

The Operations Section Chief, a member of the General Staff, is responsible for the management of all operations directly applicable to the primary mission. The Operations Chief activates and supervises organization elements in accordance with the Incident Action Plan and directs its execution. The Operations Chief also directs the preparation of unit operational plans; requests or releases resources; makes expedient changes to the Incident Action Plan as necessary; and reports such to the Incident Commander. Depending on the extent of the Incident Management team needed, this area of management may also have under its purview a Branch Director, Division/Group Supervisor, Strike Team/Task Force Leader, Single Resource Coordinator, and Staging Area Manager.

The Planning Section Chief is responsible for the collection, evaluation, dissemination, and use of information about the development of the incident and status of resources. Information is needed to: (1) understand the current situation, (2) predict probable course of incident events, and (3) prepare alternative strategies and control operations for the incident. This section serves as the Incident Commander's "clearing house" for information. The Section Chief's goal is to plan ahead of current events and to identify the need

Incident Management Team

RESOURCE:				
CATEGORY:	Resource Management		**KIND:**	Team
MINIMUM CAPABILITIES:	**TYPE I**	**TYPE II**	**TYPE III**	**TYPE IV**	**OTHER**
COMPONENT	**METRIC**				

for resources before they are needed. Depending on the extent of the Incident Management team needed, this area of management may also have under its purview a Resources Unit Leader, Situation Unit Leader, Documentation Unit Leader, Demobilization Unit Leader, and Technical Specialists.

The Logistics Section Chief is responsible for providing facilities, services, and material in support of the incident, and is accountable for all personnel working in the hazard zone of the incident. The Section Chief participates in development and implementation of the Incident Action Plan and activates and supervises the Branches and Units within the Logistics Section. Depending on the extent of the Incident Management team needed, this area of management may also have under its purview a Service Branch Director, Support Branch Director, Facilities Unit Leader, and Ground Support Unit Leader.

The Finance/Administration Section Chief is responsible for all financial, administrative, and cost analysis aspects of the incident and for supervising members of the Finance/Administration section. Depending on the extent of the Incident Management team needed, this area of management may also have under its purview a Time Unit Leader, Procurement Unit Leader, Compensation/Claims Unit Leader, and Cost Unit Leader.

Source: FIRESCOPE, California Department of Emergency Services, 2001

FEMA

RESOURCE: Individual Assistance Disaster Assessment Team

CATEGORY:	Resource Management		KIND:	Team	

MINIMUM CAPABILITIES:					
COMPONENT	METRIC	TYPE I	TYPE II	TYPE III	TYPE IV	OTHER
Personnel	See Note 1	1 IA Disaster Assessment Team leader 1 Disaster Recovery Center leader and team based on determination of number(s) of DRCs 1 Voluntary Agency Liaison 1 Donations Management leader				
Equipment		Laptop with wireless Internet capabilities Satellite or cell phone Standardized donations management, unmet needs, resource booklet Various programs and form templates for personalizing to disaster				

COMMENTS:	**Note 1:** Number based on size and scope of disaster and estimated assistance needs; knowledge.
	Team responsible for providing expert assessments of the disaster situation pertaining to claims for individual assistance and other programs. Disaster Recovery Center leader and team leader must have knowledge of all State programs and how they work with their Federal counterparts, must have worked as DRC State representative in one Federal disaster. Team members must have good knowledge of all State programs.
	All members must possess the ability to work with the public and understand disaster clients' dynamics in helping them achieve adequate service delivery.
	This team is not part of the Incident Command System, but rather is a specialty team that may be called on during times of need.

RESOURCE:		Individual Assistance Disaster Assessment Team Leader			
CATEGORY:	Resource Management		**KIND:**	Personnel	
MINIMUM CAPABILITIES:					
COMPONENT	**METRIC**	**TYPE I**	**TYPE II**	**TYPE III**	**TYPE IV**	**OTHER**
Personnel	See Note 1	Completed mission as administrative lead on 2 federally declared disasters as IA Team leader. Extensive knowledge of all programs (see comments for specifics) as well as assisted writing SAP- completed 10 years in EM in Human Services position	Completed mission as administrative lead on federally declared disasters as IA Team leader. Good knowledge on all programs (see comments for specifics), completed 5 years in EM in Human Services position	Completed mission as IA lead team member on federally declared disasters. Working knowledge on all programs (see comments for specifics), completed 3 years in EM in Human Services position	Completed mission as any member of an IA team on federally declared disasters. Attended classes on all programs (see comments for specifics)	
Equipment		Laptop with wireless Internet capabilities	Equipment provided by requesting State	Equipment provided by requesting State		
COMMENTS:	Individual responsible for leading the individual assistance disaster assessment team. (See Individual Assistance Disaster Assessment Team) Possesses an administrative knowledge of IA areas: Complete understanding of the State's other needs; assistance-State administrative plan, good working knowledge of NEMIS program. Administrative knowledge of the immediate/regular Crisis Counseling program, Manufactured Housing program, IA Housing program. Programmatic/administrative knowledge of SBA disaster loans, IRS disaster program, USDA food stamps/commodities disaster program, legal aid, Farm Services, Administration on Aging Services. Ability to work with personnel issues, as well as work closely with the public information department. This team is not part of the Incident Command System, but rather is a specialty team that may be called on during times of need.				
	Note 1: Completed Following Trainings: FEMA IA, Vol. Management, Donation Management				

FEMA

RESOURCE:		Mobile Communications Center (Also referred to as "Mobile EOC")				
CATEGORY:	Communication (ESF #2)			KIND:	Vehicle	
MINIMUM CAPABILITIES:						
COMPONENT	METRIC	TYPE I	TYPE II	TYPE III	TYPE IV	OTHER
Vehicle	Chassis	48'-53' custom trailer, bus chassis, conventional cab/van chassis, or diesel motorhome chassis with or without slide-out room	35'-40' motorhome chassis with or without slide-out room	25'-35' Gas or diesel motorhome chassis, or custom trailer (trailer does require additional tow vehicle)	Converted SUV or Travel Trailer, or 25'-40' custom built trailer (trailer does require additional tow vehicle)	
Equipment	Interior	6-10 workstations, with private meeting area for Command personnel	4-6 workstations, with private meeting are for Command personnel	2-4 workstations	1 to 2 workstations	
Equipment	Radio Frequency Transceivers	RF Communications with adjoining agencies, State agencies through mutual aid transceiver and any other frequencies	RF Communications with adjoining agencies, State agencies through mutual aid transceiver and any other frequencies	RF Communications with adjoining agencies, State agencies through mutual aid transceiver	RF Communications within jurisdiction and with adjoining agencies	
Equipment	Internet Access Speed High-Speed Fax Speed	High bandwidth capabilities via satellite such as INMARSAT or V-Sat	High bandwidth capabilities via satellite such as INMARSAT or V-Sat; Faxing through cell or satellite system (4,800 bps)	Cellular system; Faxing through cell or satellite system (4,800 bps)	Via cellular system (portable)	
Equipment	Type of system See Note 1	PBX office-style telephone system & Cellular PBX System (ML500 or similar)	PBX office-style telephone system & Cellular PBX System (ML500 or similar)	PBX office-style telephone system	Through individual cell phones only	
Equipment	On-Scene Video Monitoring	Through camera/video system	Through camera/video system			
Equipment	Computer-Assisted Dispatch	Yes	Yes	Yes		

RESOURCE:	Mobile Communications Center (Also referred to as "Mobile EOC")			
CATEGORY:	Communication (ESF #2)		KIND:	Vehicle

MINIMUM CAPABILITIES:		TYPE I	TYPE II	TYPE III	TYPE IV	OTHER
COMPONENT	METRIC					
Equipment	Computer/ Server Capabilities	Same as Type III	Same as Type III	Hardwired and wireless LAN. Workstations should have Ethernet connection and 120 vac protected receptacle. All computer based software packages pre-installed	Basic computer systems only (power source must be provided from outside vehicle)	
Personnel	Function	Same as Type II **except:** Driver/Operator with CDL certification	Same as Type III plus: IT Support Communications Support	Same as Type IV	Driver/Operator	
Personnel	Deployment Capabilities	See Note 2	See Note 2	See Note 2	See Note 2	

COMMENTS:	Radio Frequency Transceivers—Every agency has their assigned RF equipment in use. These frequencies should be distributed throughout the unit along with the most used adjoining agency transceivers. A central Communications rack should be built near the Communications Officer position. This rack should contain less used adjoining agency radios and programmable radios, giving the unit the ability to communicate with as many agencies as possible. Type I & II units should have an Interoperability Module installed in addition to the central rack. This module will allow for different frequency transceivers to communicate commonly.
	Satellite Systems—NMARSAT system can be utilized for telecommunications and DOD secure data transfer. For a MCC the unit should be roof mounted and auto-tracking. Useful for video-teleconferencing, high quality voice transmission, faxing, and dial-up Internet access. V-Sat systems use roof-mounted auto-deploy, auto-tracking dishes, and allow large downloads of bandwidth. This bandwidth can be managed to provide Internet access, voice communications, and video transfer for sending live on-scene video back to an EOC or other location. The FCC continues to approve new technology for this system. Iridium, Global Star, or other Sat-phones are ideal for in-the-field communications.
	Microwave Units—Some States and jurisdictions have microwave-capable facilities and equipment installed for quality video transfer.
	Server Computers—A rack-mounted Server should be installed in Type I, II, and III units. This Server can be designed to mimic many of the operations and software in use at the EOC. A hard-wired LAN and a wireless LAN should also be installed to enable all workstations access to the Server.
	Telephone System—An office-style PBX system should be installed in Type I, II, and III units. This system can be integrated with landlines, cell lines, and satellite telephones. Each workstation should have a telephone unit as well as units on-hand for exterior operations.
	Cellular PBX System (ML500 or similar)—This unit is used for multiple cell lines (suggest 5). It is tied into the main PBX for distribution throughout unit. The unit has auto-detect sensors that check for landline first and then switch to cell if landline is not available.
	Camera and Video Systems—The unit should have an installed mast (no taller than 30' without exterior supports) and camera system with monitors in both the conference and communications area. The video system controls the multiple inputs and distributes them to the monitors. The system should support the mast and camera, display Server Computer programs, helicopter downlink, DSS, and have the capability to receive signals from additional units by plugging into exterior console.

RESOURCE:	Mobile Communications Center (Also referred to as "Mobile EOC")				
CATEGORY:	Communication (ESF #2)		KIND:	Vehicle	
MINIMUM CAPABILITIES:	TYPE I	TYPE II	TYPE III	TYPE IV	OTHER
COMPONENT	METRIC				

Video Teleconferencing N/A

Note 1: Voice Communi-cations through Landlines, Cell Lines, and Satellite.

Note 2: All types should be capable of:

- Operating in environment with little to no basic services, including no electrical service, no phone lines, and no cell towers
- Providing own power generation and fuel supply to operate a minimum of 3-4 days without refueling
- Sustaining long term deployment as well as short-term responses
- Facilitating communications between multiple agencies (Federal, State, county, and municipal agencies)
- Operating as forward EOC
- Minimal set up time
- Serving basic personnel needs such as a bathroom, mini-refrigerator, microwave, and coffee maker where space is available

Source: North American Catastrophe Service, Inc., 2003.

RESOURCE:		Mobile Feeding Kitchen (Mobile Field Kitchen)			
CATEGORY:	Food & Water (ESF #11)		**KIND:** Equipment		
MINIMUM CAPABILITIES:					
COMPONENT	**METRIC**	**TYPE I**	**TYPE II**	**TYPE III**	**TYPE IV**	**OTHER**

COMPONENT	METRIC	TYPE I	TYPE II	TYPE III	TYPE IV	OTHER
Personnel	Number of people unit is capable of feeding	Feeds up to 1,000 twice daily	Feeds up to 650 twice daily	Feeds up to 300 twice daily	Feeds up to 100 twice daily	
Equipment	1 Mobile Kitchen Trailer (MKT-I)	45-53' trailer	36-42' trailer	20-30' trailer	16-18' trailer (concession type)	
Vehicle	See Note 1	Yes	Yes	Yes	Yes	
Personnel	Number of Kitchen Support Personnel	4, including kitchen supervisor	3, including kitchen supervisor	2	2	

COMMENTS:	The Mobile Feeding Kitchen (Mobile Field Kitchen or Rapid Deployment Kitchen) is a containerized kitchen that can be positioned forward in fulfillment of ESF #11. The units are used to support feeding operations at emergency incidents. It should be capable of providing hot meals twice daily to 650 to 1,000 individuals, either those providing the emergency response or those displaced by the disaster.
	Note 1: 2 1/2-Ton or 5-Ton Truck and Driver for Transport (1 Truck + Driver).
	The system should be equipped to provide storage, refrigeration, sanitation, and other essentials for all types of meal preparation. The units may be fitted with convection and conventional ovens, steam and tilt skillets, and modern burner units.
	The kitchens may come with a support trailer that carries tables, chairs, additional implements, tents or dining hall facilities as requested. The kitchen should provide a minimum of 360 square feet of food preparation and serving areas protected from natural elements of the environment.
	All food preparation equipment, the electrical supply, the environmental control system, and all related controls should be included. Setup and tear down should be accomplished in approximately 45 minutes.

RESOURCE:	Public Assistance Coordinator				
CATEGORY:	Information & Planning (ESF #5)			**KIND:** Personnel		
MINIMUM CAPABILITIES:					**OTHER**
COMPONENT	**METRIC**	**TYPE I**	**TYPE II**	**TYPE III**	**TYPE IV**	
Personnel	Training See Note 1	Public Assistance Coordinator (PAC) Basic Training, on-the-job training and CE Attending Scoping Meetings and FEMA State PA meetings	Trainee Public Assistance Coordinator (PAC) Basic Required Training, CE and on-the-job training for an average of 2 disasters. Assisted a PAC on the average 2 disasters Attend applicant briefings and kick-off meetings	Project Officer (PO) Basic Training CE, and on-the-job training Prepare PWs Attend applicant briefings and kick-off meetings	Trainee Project Officer (PO) Basic Required Training and on-the-job training for an average of 2 disasters. Assisted a PO on the average 2 disasters Attend applicant briefings and kick-off meetings	
		Same as Type II	Same as Type III	Same as Type IV		
Equipment					Laptop/wireless Internet capabilities Satellite/or cell phone GPS General Office Supplies Standard Forms All-weather equipment and clothing	
COMMENTS:	The Public Assistance Coordinator (PAC) is a subsection of the Public Assistance Team (PAT). The PAC is assigned to work with a Public Assistance (PA) applicant from declaration to funding approval. Posses an in-depth working knowledge of disaster relief laws, regulations, and Public Assistance programs and recovery roles of government and the private sector. Must have working knowledge of Project Worksheets preparation and validation, environmental and flood plain regulations, insurance requirements, Preliminary Damage Assessment, and 406 Mitigation. Capable of representing FEMA and officiating at public meetings and managing Project Officers and support staff. Working knowledge of NEMIS. Leadership, management, communication, organizational, interpersonal, and cognitive skills are required. The PAC performs functions of public assistance involving seven categories of eligible work as well as working with public officials on several areas of responsibility. This team is not part of the Incident Command System, but rather is a specialty team that may be called on during times of need. Note 1: Basic Required Training: • Recovery Operation I and II; Debris Management and Technology Security • Continuing Education (CE) as example Environmental and Historical Preservation • 406 Hazard Mitigation;					

RESOURCE: Public Assistance Coordinator

CATEGORY:	Information & Planning (ESF #5)		KIND:	Personnel	
MINIMUM CAPABILITIES:					
COMPONENT	**METRIC**	**TYPE I**	**TYPE II**	**TYPE III**	**TYPE IV**	**OTHER**
		• PA Cost Estimating Format • On-the-Job Training				

RESOURCE:		Rapid Needs Assessment Team				
CATEGORY:		Resource Management		KIND:	Team	
MINIMUM CAPABILITIES:		TYPE I	TYPE II	TYPE III	TYPE IV	OTHER
COMPONENT	METRIC					
Personnel	Management Element	Team Leader FEMA Representative				
Personnel	Assessment Element	HazMat Specialist Medical Specialist Mass Care Specialist Infrastructure Specialist Fire/US&R				
Personnel	Support Element	Telecomm Specialist Logistics Specialist Operations Specialist				
Equipment	Deployment Equipment	Personal Kit Resupply Kit Team Life Support Kit Team Admin. Kit Vehicle Kit Communications Support Kit Fly-Away Kit				
COMMENTS:		Number Determined by Size of Event. Determined by Number of Personnel Deployed with Team There is only one type of RNA Team. Variations may exist and/or specialists may be added according to the type and scale of disaster. Provides a rapid assessment capability immediately following a major disaster or emergency. The RNA Team will collect and provide information to determine requirements for critical resources needed to support emergency response activities. The Team is responsible for assessing both overall impact of a disaster event, and determining State and/or Federal immediate response requirements. • Management Element–supervises and coordinates the assessment process and team logistical support. • State Team Leader–maintains overall responsibility for RNA Team operations, knowledgeable of local assets, geographic information, information management systems, State				

RESOURCE:	Rapid Needs Assessment Team			
CATEGORY:	Resource Management		**KIND:**	Team
MINIMUM CAPABILITIES:				
COMPONENT	**METRIC**	**TYPE I**	**TYPE II**	**TYPE III**	**TYPE IV**	**OTHER**

response plans and procedures, State assets, response philosophies, etc.

- FEMA Representative Assessment Element–members of the assessment element are cross-trained in more than one ESF, enabling them to assess immediate needs and requirements in more than one functional area.

- HazMat Specialist (representing ESF #10)–assesses the affected sites and facilities and their potential for public exposure, identifies unsafe areas and types of hazards, contamination threats, and local hazardous materials mutual aid response capability.

- Medical Specialist (representing ESF #8)–assesses the health/medical infrastructure including hospital and primary care systems, pharmacy systems, special population needs, environmental health, sanitation issues, emergency medical services, and patient evacuation needs and capabilities.

- Mass Care Specialist (representing ESF #6, 11)–assesses the status of needs for mass feeding and emergency mass shelters, bulk distribution of relief supplies, emergency first aid needs, potential secondary disaster effects, and State and local governmental volunteer capability.

- Infrastructure Specialist (representing ESF #3)–assesses the status of transportation.

- Fire/Urban Search & Rescue (representing ESF #4, 9)–assesses the status of fire and search and rescue services including capabilities and limitations of any existing mutual aid agreements. Also identifies immediate needs for fire and/or search and rescue services.

- Support Element (QRS)–provides documentation, logistics, and communications support for the Management and Assessment elements.

- Telecommunications Specialists–installs, operates, and maintains the communications support package and provides technical support to the team during deployment.

- Logistics Specialist–provides logistical support and services for the team during all phases of team activity.

- Operations Specialist–collects assessment data from the Assessment Element, compiles data into report formats, and transmits reports to required individuals and organizations.

Source: FEMA Rapid Needs Assessment Team Operations Manual, April 2001

RESOURCE:	Shelter Management Team				
CATEGORY:	Mass Care (ESF #6)		KIND:	Team	
MINIMUM CAPABILITIES:					
COMPONENT	METRIC	TYPE I	TYPE II	TYPE III	TYPE IV	OTHER
Personnel	Shelter Supervisor	X	X	X		
Personnel	Medical Services Manager	X				
Equipment	Operations Manager (water, sanitation, power, structural)	X	X			
Vehicle	Food Services Manager	X				
Supply	Exposure Control Monitor (depends on type of event)	Optional	Optional	Optional		
COMMENTS:	Number Determined by Size of Shelter Operations				

The Shelter Management Team provides the managerial and operation support for a shelter used to house, feed, counsel, provide first aid, and related social services and welfare activities required to assist the victims of an emergency. Responsibilities of the team may include all or some of the following: operating the shelter; establishing security; ensuring the availability of adequate care, food, sanitation, and first aid; selecting and training personnel to perform operational tasks; monitoring contamination; performing decontamination; establishing exposure control and monitoring; monitoring overpressure and filtration systems; performing post-event reconnaissance; and directing egress.

RESOURCE:		Volunteer Agency Liaison				
CATEGORY:	Volunteers & Donations			KIND:	Team	
MINIMUM CAPABILITIES:		TYPE I	TYPE II	TYPE III	TYPE IV	OTHER
COMPONENT	METRIC					
Personnel	Experience, Training, Knowledge	Has TTT-Training and has trained donations management and volunteer coordination. Has extensive experience in working with NVOAD agencies and MOUs. Experience in supervisory role as a VAL in 3 or more federally declared disaster situations in different States. Has complete working knowledge of IA & PA and VAL functions under FEMA/State agreement Broad understanding and great flexibility in possible models of LTRC that could be used.	Has had training in donations management and volunteer coordination. Has worked with a State VOAD on organizing donation management on non-federally declared disaster. Experience in supervisory role as a VAL in a federally declared disaster. Aware of IA and VAL functions under FEMA/State Agreement	Has had training in donations management and volunteer coordination Active in VOAD meetings. Experience in working with a VAL in a federally declared disaster.	Has had training in donations management and volunteer coordination. Has attended State VOAD meetings	
COMMENTS:		Serves as the central point between government entities and volunteer organizations in the coordination of information and activities of VOADs (Volunteer Organizations Active in Disasters) responding in times of disaster, including those services in execution of ESF # 6 – Mass Care and ESF #15 – Volunteers and Donations. Coordinates responding voluntary agency donations efforts, including handling, storage, and disbursement of donated goods and emergent volunteers who offer assistance in a disaster response. Establishes and maintains systems for emergency need, special needs, and unmet needs referrals from FEMA/State sources to and among the voluntary agencies. Closely coordinates voluntary agency activities with community relations, donations management, PIO/JIC, and other VOLAG agencies. Assist with framework and assignment of agencies to establishing the long-term recovery committees (LTRC). Working with State VOAD's leadership, establish frequent coordination meetings with VOAD agencies during the response phase of the disaster and continued scheduling of meetings to transition to the LTRC.				

www.ingramcontent.com/pod-product-compliance
Lightning Source LLC
Chambersburg PA
CBHW080741290526
45790CB00008B/3271